Simple Sutras

Mathew "Huck" Ingles

ISBN: 1502779862
ISBN-13:9781502779861

DEDICATION

Thank you to my wife Angela for encouraging me.
Thank you to the Creator for inspiring me. Thank
you to my students for teaching me.

CONTENTS

INTRODUCTION

You won't find any yoga poses in this book. There are no pictures of yogis with their feet behind their heads. You will find no instructions on how to balance on your hands. No rubber mats, flattering stretchy pants, or Om tattoos. No medical advice, or tips to improve your running or surfing skills. No alignment or anatomy references. No chants, no deities, and no recipes. What you will find is the ancient instruction book and owners manual for a human mind.

We all want to be happy, don't we? We know that much, for sure. What's debatable is how, and by what means we get there. No one should ever claim that they have the one true answer. What leads one to happiness may not work for another. The yoga sutras are not a "key to happiness." They are a logical attempt to map out the truth about our minds, our existence, and the human condition in general. They aren't a map to the gem of happiness. Instead, like any good spiritual teaching, the sutras are a tool for uncovering that gem for ourselves.

The practice of yoga is for everyone, not just flexible people. It's not a religion. It's not just an exercise. It's a philosophy. Yoga is for old, young, boy, girl, rich, poor, sick, or well people. If you can breathe, you can learn to practice yoga.

Nowadays, when we think of yoga, we think of flexing and bending our way around a mat with a bunch of other people in an empty room with hardwood floors, but that is just part of it, and not at all the whole picture. Yoga is a philosophy of union. Yoga is a practice of behavior and meditation that brings us to better awareness of body, mind, and spirit, and ultimately to the union of all those things with the Big-Everything.

Yoga isn't about a hard workout; it's not really about a workout at all, although keeping a strong body may be an important part of it. Yoga is a way to discover and maintain awareness of our true nature and the nature of everything. Yoga helps us find ourselves. With practice and awareness, we develop healthier bodies, minds, and spirits.

The physical practice of yoga as we know it stems from Vedic traditions of India. The philosophy of yoga, which the physical practice is rooted in, can be found in many ancient and modern texts. To me, the Yoga Sutras of Patanjali is the most predominant, and a logical starting point. I really fell in love with the yoga sutras, and I wrote this book because I thought we needed a basic, down-to-earth, modernized version.

I don't have a degree in yoga. I have no degree in philosophy, either. I am not an authority; I am a reporter telling you what I have seen so far on my journey. I wrote this book from my heart. I decided to translate the sutras because I couldn't find a translation that I thought could speak to the masses. I wanted a version for the modern person.

With the help of Sanskrit-to-English dictionaries, I worked out a word-for-word translation, as best as I could. No doubt, I influenced it, even though that was not my goal. Some of what I ended up with is very common to what you will find in other translations, and some of it may be a radical new perspective. I aimed to tell the truth, simply and honestly, in a way that anyone could understand. You must not believe a word I say. Go and find out for yourself; go, see if the things I write are true. This way, you will know for sure what the truth is – and it may be very different than mine.

I always knew I was going to be a seeker. I've always wanted to know more about everything I come across. The first eastern philosophy book I remember reading was "Journey of Awakening" by Ram Dass. I was about fifteen, and although I'm sure I didn't understand much of it, it set a fire in my mind. The first time I read the Bagavad Gita, I was about eighteen. It was this giant, heady version, and while it inspired me, I really didn't get it. After finding the right version years later, it's one of my favorite books. Into my twenties came a lot of Buddhist philosophy from the Dalai Llama and Thich Nhat Hahn, who I still enjoy reading. I read and re-read the Buddhist Bible, which is a rich compilation of some pretty deep Buddhist stuff. It blew my mind. I read later that it was the book Jack Kerouac was reading right before he set off on his adventure that later inspired the classic hippie-seeker book *On the Road*. I had a few on-the-road years myself, traveling around the country homeless, camping a lot, working here and there, and living a generally peace-loving-hippie lifestyle.

During those early spiritual and philosophical explorations, I was sure many times that I had stumbled across the answer to the "Big-Everything," but I was just ignorant, much as I am today, embracing the experience of exploration. Once, out in the New Mexico desert, I ate too many mushrooms and sat in a hot spring all night under a full moon. By morning, I was pretty sure I'd been talking to aliens. In a sweat lodge, another time, I thought I had left my body and travelled around without it.

In contrast, during a two-year stay in a primitive adobe house in the Rocky Mountains, I sat and meditated on a mountainside for hours at a time, almost daily. There, I had some of my deepest moments. The more we know about, the less we understand. I lived there with almost nothing, making my life as simple as possible. I felt profoundly close to the truth.

The older I get, the more I realize I don't know. I have settled down nowadays. I don't do crazy things anymore, not nearly as often anyway. I practice and teach yoga, read, play outdoors, and spend time with my family on our little farm. I feel much more at ease now, not knowing everything about the universe, and don't have as much of the "seeker's wanderlust" that I used to have. But I still read and study daily about the human condition.

I cannot tell you what the absolute goal of yoga is, because the goal is all about YOUR true nature, and I don't know what that is. What I can tell you is that yoga makes me feel more "real," more present, and more soul-aware. When you start practicing yoga, health of your body is the most basic, immediate benefit, but health of your mind quickly follows. Then, your mood becomes more content, your mind becomes more at ease, and your life becomes a happier place.

1
WHAT ARE THE YOGA SUTRAS?

The sutras are said to be written by a sage named Patanjali. Not much is known about Patanjali, or even the true origins of the sutras. It seems to be a fragment of an ancient record of Indian science and philosophy. Most of the translations we deal with are from the versions written in Sanskrit, which explains all the crazy language yoga teachers use. It is thought that the sage Patanjali lived and wrote the sutras some 1500-2500 years ago, give or take a couple hundred years. Patanjali supposedly also wrote other works on science and health, but very little of his other work has been found.

Reading the sutras can be a beautiful and difficult task. It was not written for beginners – it was written to be read by those who already knew the practice, like Cliff's Notes. The most common form of the sutras viewed today is an outline of sorts, derived from the translations, as opposed to a direct translation itself. It is referred to as the Eight Limbs of Raja Yoga, or Ashtanga (eight limbs) yoga of Patanjali, or Classical Yoga. There are many variations of the outline. The eight limbs are contained in the translation of the sutras, but they are a bit hard to dig out, and not really the entire focus of the text. But they do make a nice quick reference to the yoga philosophy, practice, and lifestyle. The eight Limbs in Sanskrit are yamas, niyamas, asana, pranayama, pratyahara, dharana, dhyana, and samadhi. From my heart, I offer you my interpretation. It may seem a bit complicated if you are not familiar with the sutras yet. Come back to it after you start to get the hang of the yoga, and it will be a much clearer meditation checklist.

The Eight Ways to Practice Yoga

1. Practice these five right outward actions. (yamas)
   - Do no harm. Be kind. (ahimsa)
   - Be honest and truthful. (satya)
   - Restrain from stealing or cheating. (asteya)
   - Behave in a holy and respectful way, especially with love and relationships. (brahmacharya)
   - Do not possess or hoard people or objects. (aparigraha)

2. Practice these five right inward actions. (niyamas)
   - Keep the mind and body clean and healthy. (saucha)
   - Be content with the way things are. (santosha)
   - Work hard and practice discipline. (tapas)
   - Study the self, and read holy texts. (svadhyaya)
   - Surrender to a higher power. (isvarapranidhana)

3. Practice moving and seated poses for a strong body and mind. (asana)

4. Practice controlling your breathing and emotional energies. (pranayama)

5. Practice withdrawing your senses form the world and being still. (pratyahara)

6. Practice focusing your senses on one thing. Like a leaf, or a candle, or a steam, or God. (dharana)

7. Practice removing all other things from your mind except the object of meditation and you. (dhyana)

8. Practice this until you are fused with, and only aware of, the object of meditation and nothing else. (samadhi)

2
YAMAS AND NAYAMAS

The Yamas: The yamas are five actions we should keep in mind when dealing with the world. This is Patanjali's outline on what a good mental attitude, perspective, and behavior should be like. The yamas, in Sanskrit, are ahimsa, satya, asteya, brahmacharya, and aparigraha.

Yama One, Ahimsa: Do not harm. To many yogis, this means vegetarian or vegan diets. To others, it means refraining from violence, or not polluting the planet, or not hurting people's feelings. These are all acts of ahimsa, the act of non-harming. What means "non-harming" to you may not mean that to someone else. Patanjali offers no absolute rules because he wants you to use your wisdom to decide for yourself. When practicing the act of not harming, use your wisdom to determine what that means to you. How will you refrain from causing harm? It's important to note that "himsa" means harm, and "a" before it means "opposition." So in a sense, it's not enough to do no harm, we are in fact obligated to actually work to oppose harm by doing good! If we are not making love, we are making war. If we are not part of the solution, we are part of the problem.

Yama Two, Satya: Tell the truth. Satya is the act of honesty. We may think of ourselves as completely honest people, but are we? No, not likely. We all twist the truth a little, sugar coating things we don't want to tell people, and, most of all, we lie to ourselves frequently. We all have moments of "brutal honesty," when we say something we are feeling; however, when we speak too harshly, without thinking things through, we can hurt someone else's feelings. That's harming, and not a good practice of the first yama, ahimsa! If we were truly and completely honest about how we feel all the time, we may not have any friends! We must mind the first yama, and remember the act of not harming, not even with words. We must use wisdom to make good decisions that guide us to speaking the correct truth in the wisest way possible.

Yama Three, Asteya: Do not steal. We all know stealing is wrong, but we may not recognize all the ways we do it. We may steal time, or even the attention of another. Asteya is the action of non-covetousness. Yes, we know it's bad to steal our friend's money, but we might not think about the effects of stealing her time or mental capacity. On a deeper level, it is harmful to our spirits if we spend time desiring what isn't ours or desiring what we might never be able to obtain.

Yama Four, Brahmacharya: Brahmacharya means to "act Godly," to "walk with God," or to behave in a respectful way. Very often, this yama is translated to mean celibacy. And yes, at times in some people's lives, celibacy may be part of their spiritual growth or healing. But brahmacharya means much more. It means that we have to be honest in all our dealings. It means to act with integrity, and to apply the other yamas to all your actions in life. In other words, when it comes to sex, or food, or work, or business, or *anything*, we must not harm, lie, or steal. We must be honest, and we must act in a respectful way. Whatever you do in life, try to do it in a sacred way.

Yama Five, Aparigraha: Practice non-possessiveness. Aparigraha means "not grasping." I find it funny how this yama receives so little attention in a culture so fascinated with yoga. The same radical minimalist schools of yoga that felt that ahimsa meant a vegan diet, and that brahmacharya meant celibacy, felt that aparigraha meant that you should possess nothing. Many monks give up all belongings to advance their spiritual growth.

In today's society, with our absolute and total reliance on our belongings, we don't want to discuss or even think about what it would be like to live without them. But aparigraha doesn't have to mean giving up all that we have, although that may be right for you! It is the idea that we need to treat things we do possess with respect. Possessing what we don't need or don't appreciate is not a good practice of Aparigraha.

We often live life in a state of want for what we don't have, or in a desire for something to be different than it is. This desire can become overwhelming, causing a person to behave poorly, living in a constant state of dissatisfaction. Non-desire is not to be confused with complacency. It means simply to refrain from becoming a victim of the stress of desire. It's about not allowing desire to take control of you, becoming a dominant emotion. We don't have to avoid the things we love or enjoy, to practice this yama, we just have to explore our emotions and feelings towards those things, and make sure that the desire for them is not harming us or others. Grasping things can slow us down and trip us up on the path. What we grasp with our hands doesn't matter nearly as much as what we grasp with our hearts. Give love and time to the right things in life. Don't waste your attention.

The Niyamas: The Niyamas are five "inward actions" – actions we should mind when dealing with ourselves. They are saucha, santosha, tapas, svadhyaya, and isvarapranidhana.

Niyama One, Saucha: Simply put, this means cleanliness. As living humans, we have the responsibility to keep our bodies and minds clean and functioning. What we eat can be good or not good, which affects our health. We also eat with our eyes, and ears. What we read, watch, or entertain ourselves with becomes part of us, and affects our mental health. Saucha includes being mindful of what our minds ingest, actively taking care to feed it good things. Doing things we know to be bad for us, like ingesting harmful things, or overindulging, is not good practice of saucha.

Niyama Two, Santosha: Santosha is the practice of contentment, or satisfaction. It means to be satisfied with what you have. It's very easy to want more, but wanting more will always leave us dissatisfied. Dissatisfaction will often lead to unhappiness. When we are glad to have what we have, and we appreciate all the good little things in our lives, it makes us feel rich. We become content and happy. Counting our blessings leads to being happy. Expectation is the mother of disappointment.

Niyama Three, Tapas: Tapas is motivation, internal fire, discipline, or self-control. Tapas is the ability to drive yourself forward, to motivate yourself to do what you need to do. Tapas is an internal driving force that keeps you alive and going! Tapas brings up the prana. Prana is the fire of life that keeps the bugs from devouring you, the sun from drying you up, and the wind from blowing you away!

Niyama Four, Svadhyaya: Svadhyaya is the study of self, texts, and anything that helps bring you to a state of joyful enlightenment. Read things that feed your soul. Study things that support your path. Study yourself so you can better understand yourself. Study the natural world and its people, so you can better understand who, what, and where you are.

Niyama Five, Isvarapranidhana: To surrender to a higher power. The word "God" can mean a lot of different things to different people. What "God" means to you is a very, very personal thing, as it should be. To me, God is the sum of all things, the total of everything known and unknown. To me nothing can be left out – all things are within God. To you, it is whatever your heart tells you it is. Isvarapranidhana can simply mean "to surrender yourself to something bigger than you." We all understand that we are not the ruler of the universe; that something, if not many things, are greater than us. The sun, the stars, the earth – many things are greater than us, and do not rely on us. They are beyond our control as an individual. But as humans, we tend to kid ourselves a bit about what we have control over. It's easy for us to think that we are able to control others, or that we have the ability to change things that we cannot indeed change. Isvarapranidhana is an invitation to free yourself from the responsibility of trying to control every aspect of your life. Once we let go, we have peace.

3
A WORD ABOUT ASANA

Asana is the physical practice of yoga. Asana literally means, "a seated position." The physical practice of yoga as we know it today stemmed from the practice of seated meditation. It became obvious to the ancients that sitting in meditation for long periods was not possible if your body was not strong and healthy. When we realize that the body is a vessel for the mind and soul, we feel the need to keep it in good working order. The yoga postures that we practice today were designed to keep the body strong, healthy, and limber so that we can feel healthy and happy. As you have noticed, there are no pose instructions in this book. But that doesn't mean that yoga classes are not part of this practice. The sutras were written to give us a guide to the mind of yoga, and a good yoga class will help us with the physical part. Do you have to practice yoga poses to be a yogi? No. Does it help you make peace with yourself? Yes.

Find a yoga teacher you like. Try lots of different styles. Find a physical practice that is well matched to your mental practice. My physical practice is very much part of my yoga. But, without the philosophy, it would just be stretching to me.

4
THE SUTRAS OF PATANJALI

I translated the words of Patanjali to the best of my ability. As I've stated, I am not a scholar, but a yogi who is passionate about the teachings with a desire for a translation that everyone can comfortably read. In making this translation, I used dictionaries, other translations, and my intuition and experience, to create what I felt was the most simple, straightforward version. The text is traditionally broken up into four books. Each book is traditionally broken into individual points, or sutras. The word "sutra" has the same root meaning as "sew" or "suture." As such, they are small stitches of information that hold together a larger idea. In this translation, Patanjali's words are written after each sutra number and my commentary follows, written in italics.

5
BOOK ONE: THE WAY OF YOGA

1.1   The following is the way of yoga.

1.2   Yoga is the practice of calming the waves of the mind.

This is Patanjali's definition of yoga. Our minds are constructed of "waves" caused by mental impressions. These waves influence how we think and feel. They can cloud our judgment, causing us to misperceive things, or they can help us understand the world around us.

1.3   Once the mind waves are calmed, the practitioner identifies with her or his own true self.

This is peace! This is "enlightenment!" The moment that we are able to calm the mind waves, even just a little bit, we are able to see true selves. Truly knowing ourselves is the key to contentment in this life. Once we have a clear view of ourselves, and we know where we are thinking from, we get a better, more "true" view of the world. It's like finding your soul.

1.4   When the mind waves are not calm, the practitioner identifies with the fluctuating mind waves, and not the true self.

This is the opposite of the peace brought about by mental clarity. In this sutra, Patanjali explains that when we are in a state of heavy "mind waves," we think ourselves to be those waves. When I am angry, I AM angry! When I'm happy, I AM happy. In our mind's eye, we literally become the thing that we are experiencing instead of our true selves. We become our ego, and not our soul.

1.5 It is possible to identify five different causes of mind waves. Any of the five can be pleasant or unpleasant.

1.6 The five different causes are:
1) True knowledge based on fact.
2) False knowledge based on wrong information, or wrong perception.
3) Imagination, illusion, or day dreaming.
4) Sleep, or an empty mind.
5) Memories.

Patanjali starts to break it down for us in a logical way we can understand. He identifies five ways that we create the "mind waves," making it easier for us to recognize our actions in life that can bring us to seeing things clearly (or not clearly). He goes on to describe the five ways in more detail.

1.7 True knowledge comes from information obtained from an authority we trust, direct perception, or something we can test and prove to be true.

1.8   False knowledge comes from misinformation, or an incorrect perception.

1.9   Knowledge obtained from imagination, illusion, or day dreaming is without substance.

1.10   Sleep is the absence of awareness of the mind waves.

1.11   Memory is the perception of a past mental formation, as it is perceived in the present moment.

1.12   With repeated practice, one can intentionally free one's self from the mind waves, when desired.
    If we practice, we can learn to separate ourselves from the mind waves at will.

1.13   By repeated practicing of freeing one's self from the mind waves, the waves themselves will calm down.

1.14   Long, repeated, steadfast practice with awareness and renunciation is the foundational method for calming the waves of the mind. This practice is called meditation.

This is a good recipe for the mental action of meditation. We practice paying attention while letting go of our attachments. While Patanjali doesn't speak much of yoga poses, keep in mind that the practice of physical yoga is intended to be a moving meditation.

1.15   Practicing renunciation means controlling our passion towards that which we desire.

To me, this is a very important sutra. I feel that people often lose their way here. They read this sutra, or another philosophy like it, and they believe that it's telling them to give up the things they desire. Then, when they can't do it, they write the whole thing off as bull. Notice that he's saying that we are to "practice controlling our passion" – it's our passion that can cause us pain and confusion, not just the action! It's not that we shouldn't give up things that we know are bad for us. If we know them as "bad for us" then wisdom will tell us to renounce those things. But, not all things that we are passionate about are bad for us. What we have to realize is that even excessive, uncontrolled passion towards things that are good can cause us pain! It is possible to become so passionate about something that we create stress for ourselves. We identify with the mind wave of passion! Then, we are taken away from identifying with our true selves, and we do not make our best decisions, or act in the wisest of ways.

1.16   The ultimate state of this practice of awareness and renunciation is when the practitioner transcends even the awareness of the natural world, and is only aware of her or his true self, known as the soul.

Here, Patanjali gives us a glimpse of what a spiritual home run looks like. When we become well practiced, and all the cosmic tumblers fall into place, we MAY get a moment where we no longer identify with anything but our true selves – our "soul." These moments can come and go. They can last seconds, or years. I think most of us may only see small moments of this spiritual bliss. Don't be discouraged! It's the journey that counts, not the destination. That's why we are here!

1.17   This practice leads to the happiness and bliss of being truly aware of self, and aware of a state of pure being.

No ifs, ands, or buts. It's a direct statement from Patanjali. If we practice it will lead to being happy. He has faith in the practice.

1.18   While in a state of pure being, old and dormant mental impressions will often rise up and disturb the mind, again creating more mind waves.

Ah, the rollercoaster of life... So there it is. Even if we reach the blissful state of mind where we are not being affected by the mind waves, old mind waves come in and fill the void. So, what he's saying is WE ARE HUMAN! We cannot be perfect beings while in this body. We may have moments of spiritual ecstasy, but without a doubt, our own drama will pull us back into the state of misperception.

1.19   In the state of pure awareness, it is also possible for one to lose awareness of the self, and become one with the natural world.

Ever had a moment of bliss where you felt like you were woven into the fabric of the natural world? Perhaps you were watching the sun rise, swimming in a peaceful lake, playing or listening to beautiful music, making love, or working in a flower garden. He's talking about these moments – where the whole world seems beautiful, were we have no desire to be anywhere else, where we are overcome by beauty, and we feel totally at peace. Patanjali is pointing out that these, too, have potential to be meditations, to be moments of enlightenment.

1.20   We must learn to have faith in the true self discovered by this vigorous practice, noting the differences from our past spiritual experiences.

Patanjali is trying to be encouraging here. After letting us in on the harsh fact that we will no doubt fall from grace over and over, he's telling us to have faith in ourselves, and to take notice of our spiritual growth as it happens!

1.21   Vigorous practice with a positive attitude will bring you quickly to the state of mind known as yoga.

That's with a positive attitude! If you want to be a grumpy, egocentric, know-it-all yogi, you won't get anywhere fast. If you want positive things, think positive thoughts. Be a happy, easy going, flexible yogi.

1.22   Differences in speed of progression in the practice will be notable for those whose efforts are mild, moderate, or diligent.

Simply put, the more we practice, the faster we will see that spiritual maturity.

1.23   The mind waves may also be calmed by focusing on, and surrendering to, the universal and original soul, the oneness of everything, or the total sum of things seen and unseen, known by many as God.

As Patanjali was a scientist, and not a preacher, he's trying to remain politically correct here, and tap into yoga's ability to speak to many different belief systems. He's saying that meditation on God, or "prayer," is also a path to that yoga mind of self/soul awareness. He also lays out a basic definition of God that most people can agree with as the "Original Soul" or "oneness of everything." There is no doubt that Patanjali understood that the path of yoga was a path to liberation, and a way to prepare this human vessel for a connection to God. Meditation is the quiet conversation between us and the Big-Everything. Like an unspoken loving smile, we come face-to-face and heart-to-heart with truth.

He goes on, trying to appeal to our logic, to further our understanding of what he means by "God."

1:24   God is that which is supreme and totally present, free from all conflicts, and in no way affected by duality, pain, action, or location.

1.25   God is that which is the root, seed, cause, and origin of all knowledge, wisdom, and information.

1.26   God is that which is the original teacher, the absolute first, and is not bound by time in any way.

1.27   God is that which is often represented by the sacred syllable "Om."

Om, or "aum," is the original thing. It's the first sound, the first word, the base. It represents the original everything. We have om jewelry, and om clothing, and om tattoos, but do we really know what it means? Om is the representation of the basic God energy material that all things were molded from. When I hear physicists talking about looking for the "God particle" I think of om. Om is the one true building block of everything.

1.28   Practice can be the repetitious pronouncing of the sacred syllable "Om" while being aware of its meaning.

Om-ing can be a great meditation!

1.29 Meditation on the universal soul called God during practice can assist in removing obstacles to becoming aware of the true self through the state of pure being.

To understand the little picture, it helps to take a look at the big picture. If we don't feel that we can understand ourselves, then we need to better understand the Big-Everything. This is where being humble comes in. If we only work towards finding our true selves, and don't take a moment to compare ourselves to the Big-Everything, we are like a goldfish in a bowl who believes that the world begins and ends at the edge of the glass.

1.30 These obstacles to success in practice can include things like disease, mental laziness, doubt, carelessness or negligence, physical laziness, lack of moderation in pleasurable activities, living in a fantasy world, failing to learn from our actions, lack of progress, or a scattered mind.

*Can you relate to any of those things? I
know I can, and do, almost on a daily basis. These
are natural states of humanness that can cause us to
lose our way on the path of spiritual growth. In no
way does he expect us to be able to eliminate these
things from our lives. But we can learn to recognize
them, and see them when they are influencing us.
Then we develop the ability to disarm them a bit,
and lesson their frequency and ability to affect us.*

1.31   Chaotic mental waves can also be caused by
sadness or grief, despair or depression, or lack of
physical control over one's movement or breathing.

*More human afflictions… These things
happen to everyone. We get sad, we grieve for
losses, we have low moments of despair, we become
sick and have discomfort in our breath and bodies.
These discomforts can create a lot of mental chaos
and steal our peace of mind. But, just knowing that
this is possible can give us some relief. If we know
the source of the chaos, and we can identify it, we
feel more in control, and have a better shot at
finding our peace of mind again.*

1.32   Being diligent in the practice of meditation can help to overcome these obstacles.

Another shot of hope. Meditation teaches us how to navigate these crazy human minds! With practice, we can have more control. We may never have perfect control, but we can have some. Like a ship in bad weather, we may be tossed about, but we can still keep it going in the right direction.

1.33   By encouraging ourselves, through our practice, to have a mindset of friendliness and love, compassion and mercy, happiness, indifference to pleasure or pain, and indifference to praise or blame, we will develop a long lasting positive attitude.

This sutra makes me smile. This is what John Lennon meant when he said, "The love you take is equal to the love you make." If we encourage our minds to function with a good, loving attitude, we get more of the same. Our minds are creatures of habit. We often handle things the way we handled them in the past. But, we can rewrite our habits by creating new ones! In the Buddhist tradition, they call this "changing the peg." In old post-and-beam barn construction, two big beams are held together by a wooden peg pounded through a hole in both beams. Often, that peg rots before the beams do, so a new peg is put over the end of the old and pounded through, pushing the old peg out. The mind can achieve this too – we can replace rotten habits in our minds by creating new, better ways of thinking, and replacing the old ones.

1.34   We can even encourage a positive attitude by taking a good exhale and relaxing in that state of mind.

In a moment of stress, have you ever taken a good breath and a releasing sigh? Sometimes that's all we need to set ourselves right.

1.35   Or, we can even find bliss by meditating on any object of interest, and contemplating its true origin.

Find something you see as positive, beautiful, or holy, like a puppy, a flower, or something else of beauty. Then, spend time thinking about how it came to be and what makes it beautiful. Spending time in reverence of things we admire can bring us out of our own drama, and into that big picture, the Big-Everything; and before long, we can see the whole world as a beautiful thing.

1.36   We can ease or minds by concentrating on, or imagining, a beautiful bright light.

1.37   Or we can find pure being and bliss by concentrating on things that we consider enlightening, like great spiritual teachers, or objects.

In the last two sutras, Patanjali offers up some other methods for bringing ourselves to spiritual bliss. Meditating on a bright light, like the sun (don't stare at it!), the moon (stare away…), or a candle flame can work. Or, meditating on great spiritual teachers or objects of our religions can be pure yoga for many.

1.38   Or we can enlighten ourselves by meditating on things experienced during our dreams.

The ancients saw dreams as a place of great communication with the self and the divine. When we wake after having an interesting dream, whether unnerving or inspiring, it pays to sit with it for a while and meditate on its meaning.

1.39   It is possible to gain clarity by focusing on just about anything that helps you calm the waves of your mind.

This is a very open-ended statement. When we use our wisdom, and we know ourselves, we will find that just about anything that brings us to a place of peace can be a meditation.

1.40   Mastering this ability to calm and focus the mind will give you the ability to contemplate and understand things as complex as the entire universe, or as subtle as a single atom.

Meditation helps to bring a person closer to their best possible potential when it comes to wisdom. The more we meditate, the more we understand. The more we understand, the wiser we become.

1.41   With practice, the yogi begins to see that the seer, the things that we see with, and that which we see, are all one thing, and are all really her or him. The yogi's mind becomes like a pure transparent gem letting light through it, able to transmit the truth, without interference.

Mind blown! Once we start to dig into our minds we can recognize the different parts and pieces doing their jobs. We see our "self" or soul, and we notice it sees out. We see out through the mind, and our eyes, and our senses. The mind has no consciousness of its own. The mind does not see. The mind is a lens for the soul to see the world. Soul sees through mind, mind detects the world with senses, senses detect the world. At a point of peace and clarity, we may come to an incredible realization: there are no true dividing lines between these things! We can't really tell where our soul begins and our mind ends. We see that we are absolutely interconnected with everything we can perceive! In this moment of true bliss, we let go of ourselves, and become free from our own drama. We become like a clear window letting the truth go right from the source to our understanding, without interference by our usually chaotic minds. I think therefore I AM NOT! Patanjali goes on to further explain this state of "no-mind."

1.42   In this deep stage of clarity, even words, their meaning, and how we interpret them all become part of the oneness, and a sensation of true, deep understanding.

1.43   In this deep stage of mental clarity, our own memories no longer affect our insight, and we get a very true and honest view of self.

1.44   In this deep stage even the most subtle things that our minds reflect upon, or don't reflect upon, become understood.

1.45   The truly deepest and most subtle layer of practice is when our awareness of self has completely dissolved, and cannot be distinguished as separate from anything else.

In the last three sutras, Patanjali sums up the awareness of interconnectedness – the point where we realize we are all one! Us, them, you, me, the yoga mat, the studio, the water, the clouds, the sky, are all truly connected!

1.46   All these states of mind are dependent on the seed of the practice of meditation.

He reminds us again, before we get somewhere, we need to start heading there! First we are honest with ourselves about where we are, and then we begin there. We plant a "seed" and then grow a plant! We can't just buy, or find, the finished product. We need to take the journey ourselves.

1.47   The practice of the deepest forms of meditation will bring forth the purest understanding of the relationship between the manifested soul, and the universal soul.

The manifested soul is you, us, life! The universal soul is the sum of everything, the original spark, God! Patanjali is summing up the big picture for us. We practice yoga with awareness, we find the depths of ourselves, we gain understanding, and we start to see the truth about the Big-Everything!

1.48   Once you have found the state of true understanding of the reality of self, known as enlightenment, then you will experience the true intuition and insight of wisdom.

Enlightenment means enlightenment of something. It's not a merit badge for meditating, or some great mental state where we know all and see all. Enlightenment means we have "cast light" on something. We are more aware of how that thing works, whether it's how to operate a computer, grow a garden, or in this case, understand the reality of who and what and where we are! Patanjali says that once we start to get a grasp on that, we start to come into our best potential for intuition and wisdom. He's telling the truth.

1.49   Then, you will be able to distinguish true knowledge gained from this intuition, from knowledge gained from books, teachers, or inference.

When we find our true intuition and wisdom, we begin to understand things. Wisdom seems to come from within us, and from within the Universal Soul. Our connection to this intuitive wisdom is strong, and we tend to accept it as truth. We can clearly see the difference between wisdom gained from intuition, and knowledge gained from information. Our intuitive wisdom becomes a shelter for our hearts and souls. We trust it, believe it always, and never feel the need to defend it. We are enlightened of the truth. We are brought from a place of doubt to a place of love and stability.

1.50   With this new understanding, we are reborn. We are freed from the past mental impressions that caused unwanted mind waves, and no new unwanted impressions are created.

This makes my heart smile. To me this is it. This is nirvana, bliss, heaven. We are reborn. Born to understanding and freed from our drama.

1.51   In the final deepest practice, the path of understanding is surrendered, and we settle into a seedless state of true oneness and bliss.

True bliss comes when we let go of even the path that got us there. We let go of the attachment to everything we learned on our path. We let go of our attachment to the yoga practice. We let go of our attachment to our own wisdom, and we learn to just BE.

6
BOOK TWO: THE PRACTICE OF YOGA

In the first book, Patanjali took us from A-Z. In itself, the first book is a fairly thorough explanation of yoga, but we often need to hear things from a few different perspectives before we can begin to truly grasp them. So in the second book, Patanjali starts again. He begins to re-explain the path of yoga. He then provides us with the eight-step method that was set out in the beginning of this book. That eight-step method is the eight-limbed path of yoga that you may already be aware of.

2.1   Self discipline, Self study, and meditation on God are all acts of yoga.

Notice that he says they are all acts of yoga. He doesn't say that you need to do all three! You could, and many do, but, if you did only one of these things, you will still progress on the path. What he is speaking of here are the three common paths of yoga; Karma yoga, Jnana yoga, and Bakti yoga.

2.2   Practicing yoga both reduces afflictions and increases the state of pure being.

2.3   Five afflictions that can inhibit practice are:
    1) Ignorance
    2) Ego or pride
    3) Attachment
    4) Aversion
    5) Excess attachment to life, or fear of death
        A great list of possible pitfalls to watch out for! I sure see myself slipping into them often. He goes on to explain them in better detail.

2.4   Ignorance is the source of all sorrow, whether it's dormant, barely active, active without our awareness, or fully influencing us.

2.5   Ignorance is mistaking the transient, impure, painful, and non-spiritual, for the permanent, pure, joyful, and spiritual.

Nothing can cause more trouble than thinking we understand something when we really don't. And in a spiritual sense, this can be devastating. If we find a small truth, and mistake it for the big truth, we could wind up stopping our growth on the path, thinking we have arrived at the truth. Ignorance becomes one of our greatest challenges.

It's as if we set out hiking up a river to find the source of water, and as we go, our understanding grows. As the river gets smaller and smaller, we start to think, "I must be getting close to the truth about the source of this river." We follow it all the way up to the tiniest stream, to a rock where the water is just a trickle bubbling out of the ground, and we say, "I found it! I found the true source of the water in the river!" We declare that the truth, and our work is done! But, we are ignorant. We are not wise enough to look up, see the clouds dropping rain, see the water soaking the ground, and consider the bigger picture. We think we found the truth, but ignorance of the bigger picture fooled us.

2.6   Egoism is the mistaken identification of one's self with the ability to be aware.

With yoga practice, we start to become "aware of our awareness." Just like the story of the river, ignorance can trick us here into thinking we've found the source. We easily mistake our awareness of the world as our true self, as our soul. But, with further practice, we begin to see that we are much more than our ability to see, taste, touch, smell, feel, and think.

2.7   Pleasure can lead to attachment.

2.8   Hatred can lead to aversion.

Attachment and aversion can cause us trouble. It's not that we want to avoid these two emotions, it's that we want to be able to have a say on how they affect us. Patanjali is reminding us that indulging in pleasure can lead to attachments. Maybe more that we can handle. And, even more importantly, he's reminding us that indulging in dislike for things, people, ideas, behaviors, and other's beliefs can lead to the pain of aversions. I think these last two sutras are here to remind us that it's just as spiritually damaging to hate something as it is to be addicted to it. So whether you are vegan or eat meat, whether your are celibate or sexual, or whether you are for or against something doesn't matter as much as how you let the attachment and aversion affect you. You can even become addicted to being addicted to nothing.

2.9   Love for life will cause even the wisest yogi to be attached to self preservation.

All living things experience the feeling of attachment to life. We all have the desire to preserve our own lives, but this obstacle can be controlled. The more we understand life and death, the less we can fear it. The less we fear it, the better we can manage our deep-rooted fear of the unknown. We will become less selfish, less fearful, and less greedy. The opposite happens in the ignorance of life and death. A desire for self-preservation combined with the fear of death creates much of the world's suffering. Greed and hatred are founded in this ignorance.

2.10   The most subtle of these afflictions can be overcome with practice, by focusing on minimizing them.

Don't make mountains of mole hills, right?

2.11   Waves created in the mind by these afflictions can be quieted through the practice of meditation.

All we have to do is practice and we heal. It's a great thing to remember when we are overwhelmed by too many ideas, concepts, opinions, and so on. All we have to do is find our "yoga." Yoga means to connect, to link up. So whether we practice asana, the physical workout, or pranayama, prayer, chanting, seated meditation, or walking meditation, it doesn't matter. Anything that creates a link between us and the Big-Everything is yoga. Practicing will bring us where we want to go.

2.12   It is believed that the root of these afflictions are seeds left by our actions of the past. Actions we remember from this life, and possibly actions from past lives. These actions will affect our lives now, and in the future.

2.13   The roots and fruits of our actions will determine our place in life, the length of our life, and how enjoyable our lives will be.

2.14   The roots and fruits of our actions will determine whether our lives are prosperous or not, and whether our lives are enjoyable or not.

That's karma in a nutshell. The last four sutras lay out the groundwork for the basic concept of karma. Keep in mind that this is a logical perspective of a real and physical chain of events. I think westerners often see karma as a godly judgment system where if we do wrong, God writes it down and later we get a stubbed toe. But karma is more of a realization that we, and all our actions, are inter-connected. And everything we do can assist in determining the outcome of our lives. It's a way of saying that we are all responsible for our own actions, and we will reap the results of those actions.

2.15   The enlightened yogi understands that everything we experience is affected by the forces from our own mental impressions, as well as the natural fluctuations and resistance of nature, and can cause us pain or sorrow.

This is a good thing to remember. This sutra reminds us that we are not, and can never be, perfect. Patanjali is saying, as he said before, that we are affected by our mental chaos, our mind waves, but we are also affected by the natural chaos of the nature of our worldly existence. So we can control our own stuff, but not the stuff of nature. We can control ourselves, but not others. So we will always be subject to some sorrow and pain. That is the human condition.

2.16 Only pain and sorrow of the future can be avoided.

This is a warning against dwelling in the unhappiness of the past. We only have control over what is in the future.

2.17 Pain and sorrow is really caused by mistakenly identifying the soul, or that which sees, with the nature of reality, or that which is seen. This misperception should be avoided.

2.18   Understand that the brilliance of nature, your actions, your sense of being, your character, all the elements, your senses, the body and organs, and all the things you are composed of, are not you. They only exist for the joy and use of your soul, and so you can understand your true self, and the world around you.

These last two sutras are helping us dig deeper into the idea of who and what we really are, and the idea that the parts that we are made of are not really us. And even deeper, our actions are not us, and our character is not us. Even our MIND is not really the true us.

2.19   The waves, or fluctuations, of the natural world affect the soul. While affecting the soul, they can be distinguishable, or not; very obvious, or not.

The waves of the natural world – the chaos of existence – is always affecting us. We are always under the influence of some energetic action, whether we are aware of it or not.

2.20   The true seer is the soul, and is pure awareness only; even though it is aware of things, it is not those things.

Patanjali is getting heavier. Now, just a while ago he said that we are not our awareness, and now he is saying we are. Why does it seem like contradiction is starting to show up in the sutras? Patanjali is trying to help us break through one of our hardest mental layers. He wants us to grasp the very fine and fluctuating line between the atman and the world. The atman is the basic soul. It is the unstained relic of God that we all are sparked from. It has no name, no sex, no age, no ideas, and no body. By considering the nature of our own awareness, and by meditating on it over and over, we begin to get a glimpse of what we TRULY are! To me, this is one of the most profound things Patanjali is sharing.

2.21   The natural world, and our awareness, the seer and the seen, only exist to bring us to this understanding.

The whole reason we are here in this place, in this life, is to understand the nature of ourselves. We are here to find the yoga, the union between body, mind, and spirit, and ultimately, between self and God. What is the meaning of life? The meaning is to answer the question!

2.22   Once we understand that we are not what we are aware of, our actions still affect the world as they always did.

Okay, so you now understand that you are partly infinite, and you feel more empowered and able than you ever have before, DON'T GO CRAZY! All kidding aside, I really do think that's his sentiment here. Keep awareness and control over your worldly responsibilities because they still count. As your spirit rises towards the clouds, keep your feet firmly planted on the ground.

2.23   The reason that the soul and the natural world, our awareness, and that which we are aware of, have been brought together, is so that we can realize our own true nature.

2.24   Ignorance of our own true nature leads to the confusion that our soul is that which we observe.

2.25   The sense of freedom comes when we are able to overcome the illusion of the bond between seer and seen, between the awareness of the soul, and all the things it is aware of.

   Patanjali recaps in these last three sutras. He's working to help us to begin to pierce the veil, and see reality as it is.

2.26   The way to break this illusion is to wholeheartedly meditate on the truth of what you are and are not, with an attitude of discernment, and discretion.

   By adding a bit of discernment to our practice we can better start to understand the truth.

2.27   By this discriminating practice of discernment, the yogi gains true wisdom, sevenfold.

2.28   By the devoted practice of the limbs of yoga, impurities of the mind are destroyed, and the highest wisdom shines bright and beautiful.

This is where the eight limbs of yoga from the beginning of the book show up in the sutras.

2.29   The eight limbs of yoga are:
1. The outward observances, rules of behavior towards all. (yamas)
2. The inward observances, rules of behavior towards self. (niyamas)
3. Yoga poses, seated positions, and the physical practices of yoga. (asana)
4. Breath energy control. (pranayama)
5. Taking retreat, withdrawing the senses. (patyahara)
6. Practicing concentration, focusing the mind. (dharana)
7. Holding the focus, reflecting on our true nature, practicing understanding. (dhyana)
8. The union of self with the object of meditation, or the universal soul, becoming one with everything. (samadhi)

Now he breaks down the first one from above (Yamas) into five things:

2.30   The outward observances are:
1. Do no harm. (ahimsa)
2. Be truthful. (satya)
3. Do not steal. (asteya)
4. Practice restraint and self control, keep your actions holy. (brahmacharya)
5. Do not be attached to possessions. Own nothing, take nothing.(aparigraha)

2.31   These yamas are great universal vows that apply to all, regardless of place, class, or time of existence.

Everyone, no matter who they are, should adhere to the five yamas.

2.32   The inward observances are:
1. Cleanliness and healthiness. (saucha)
2. Contentment. (santosha)
3. Hard work and discipline. (tapas)

4. Study and awareness of the self through teachings. (svadhyaya)
5. Surrender to God, or to the universal wisdom. (isvarapranidhana)

2.33   If you have principals that seem to run contrary to the observances, then use your own discrimination.

Patanjali is putting the responsibility on us to determine exactly what the observances mean. He's saying that our own wisdom should be the final say as to how these apply to us.

2.34   Questionable knowledge leading to violence, aggression, and so on, is caused by greed, anger, and delusion. It always leads to endless pain and ignorance. It doesn't matter if you do it yourself, order it, cause it to be done, or allow it to happen. It doesn't matter if it's mild, moderate, or intense in degree. Work against this with your thoughts and feelings.

Good trees bare good fruit, and bad trees bear bad fruit, right? Any philosophy with intent to cause harm is ignorance, not the truth.

2.35   When a yogi's non-violent nature is firmly established, then people around her or him will give up their own violent nature. (Ahimsa)

Example is the greatest teacher. The presence of a truly non-violent person can have an incredible effect on other people, even entire nations. I think of people like Gandhi, Christ, Mother Teresa, and Martin Luther King. I think of the stories of Saint Francis, who they say could walk up to wild animals and pick them up.

2.36   When a yogi becomes firmly planted in living the truth, even her or his actions become the foundation for what is true. (Satya)

Even our basic actions become teachers. What we say is almost meaningless next to what we do. Telling the truth is one thing, but living the truth is another.

2.37　When a yogi practices taking nothing that is not theirs, or that they don't need, then precious things will be entrusted to them. (Asteya)

When we show responsibility for the little we have, we may be given the right to steward more important things. This is a fact of life.

2.38　When a yogi acts in a holy way, practicing restraint and self control, then strength, energy, and potency will be gained. (Brahmacharya)

While this sutra often refers to sexual restraint, it does not mean only that. Restraint of all behaviors and habits is part of a good practice. Celibacy is a big part of spiritual growth. At times in people's lives, it is the appropriate thing to do. Some choose to take an oath for life, and focus on spiritual growth. It can be a powerful thing! It should not be a foundation to shame people into an aversion to sex, or their bodies. We have enough guilt and shame in this world. We are natural and beautiful! Behaving in a holy way isn't just about celibacy. It refers to all our actions. Don't harm, don't lie, and don't steal; sex or otherwise. It's truly that simple.

2.39   When a yogi lets go of possessions, owns and takes nothing, then the reason we were born becomes obvious. (aparigraha)

If we don't clog up our lives with cheap plastic crap, we may have some space to see what we really are and why we are here!

2.40   When a yogi keeps the body clean and healthy, she or he no longer obsesses about gratifying one's self with physical contact from others.

2.41   When the body is clean and healthy, and the mind is cheerful, and the senses controlled, it leads to knowledge of the self. (saucha)

If we care for ourselves, love ourselves, keep ourselves healthy, and treat ourselves with respect, we are less likely to fall victim to insecurity that people often try to fill with sexual obsession. If we spend more time caring about how we feel and less time caring about whether others find us attractive or not, we will be more content. Treat yourself like a holy object, because you are!

2.42   When the yogi is content, she or he will always be very happy. (santosha)

2.43   Hard work and self discipline burn away impurities of the body and senses. (tapas)

Hard work is good for the soul. Just about every culture knows that one.

2.44   Self study leads to the realization and communion with the greatest of things, whether you see that as God, or your own savior or deity, or as the universe. (svadhyaya)

2.45   Surrendering to that greatest of things, whether God, or that which is greater than you, leads to perfection in the highest forms of meditation. (isvarapranidhana)

We all need something to surrender to. If you are an atheist, meaning you don't believe in a higher power, surrender to all that science and physics is trying to understand. Surrender to the idea that the universe is huge and unknown. If you are a Gnostic, meaning you accept that you don't know if there is a God, then surrender to the not-knowing, and realize how small we really are. If you believe in a God or higher power, then surrender into the omnipotence of that greatness.

2.46   The practice of yoga is a combination of steady awareness and happiness. (asana)

Because of our modern focus on physical yoga practice, this sutra may be one of the most commonly quoted and translated of all. I repeat this sutra, in many different ways, to my students all the time. The Sanskrit for this sutra is sthirasukhasanam. If you break it down, sthira means firmness, awareness, steadfast, or constant perseverance. Sukha means comfortable, happy, with ease, to be in a good headspace. And asana is the physical practice of yoga poses. A good meditation or yoga pose should be made of those two things.

2.47   Success in the practice of yoga is when the work to do it becomes effortless, and we are aware of the infinite soul.

To me, these are those Zen moments when we are deep in our practice, and everything is grooving together. We are joyfully there without any desire to be anywhere else. By effortless work, Patanjali doesn't mean that the pose or meditation is so easy for you that you can do it without even trying. He means that it isn't disturbing our mind waves. The pose doesn't freak us out anymore even though it's hard work. Those are the joyful, juicy moments in a yoga practice.

2.48   From that point on, the yogi is undisturbed by dualities.

Duality creates a lot of mental work for us. Am I hot or cold? Is this pose too much, or not enough? Am I happy or sad? When we hit that Zen moment in our yoga practice, whether it's asana, meditation, or a walk in the woods, we become truly content, and have no desire to check our "meters" of duality.

2.49   Once the yogi feels that the physical practice has been implemented, then they should practice breath energy control, learning to control breathing in, breathing out, and the pauses at the top and bottom of breath. (pranayama)

In asana, we practice staying calm and focused while moving. Pranayama is practicing staying focused while breathing. And ultimately, pranayama isn't simply about breathing control, it's about controlling our emotions.

2.50   Breath energy control is the skill of breathing in, breathing out, and pausing the breath, all while regulating the subtle difference in the timing.

Much like asana, there are lots of different methods for practicing pranayama. Patanjali is offering the basics. Practice in breath, out breath, and retained breath, all while staying focused and calm.

2.51   The fourth skill of breath energy control is the ability to breathe a regulated breath without any effort.

Once we practice controlling our breathing, and we can do it with some confidence, we want to be able to breathe a nice even breath without any anxiety. Breathing is the key to controlling our stress and emotions.

2.52   The practice of breath energy control removes that which covers the light of wisdom.

2.53   Then the mind is ready to concentrate in meditation.
   Breath control helps to remove some of the last subtle obstacles in the mind. Breath control is where we really learn to manage stress and anxiety.

2.54   Going into retreat, withdrawing the senses, means removing yourself from contact with the outside world, and focusing your attention inward, toward the self. (pratyahara)

2.55   This practice allows the yogi to gain control over the senses.

This is why monks and nuns live in monasteries. In order to learn to control something, we have to slow it down and have a look. If you want to understand a bee, catch it, watch it for a few minutes in a jar, and then let it go. If you want to understand how we move, breathe, think, and feel, slow it down and have a look. This is what asana practice does. Slow down our movement and have a look. To retreat is to slow down the input the world is having on your senses. Take a vacation or a walk in the park. Let just a few simple things in a time.

7
BOOK THREE: THE ACCOMPLISHMENTS OF A YOGI

3.1   Fixing the mind's awareness and attention on one point or thing is concentration. (dharana)

3.2   Keeping a steady flow of attention towards that point or thing is meditation. (dhyana)

A very good and simple definition of meditation! Concentrating on something and keeping that concentration IS meditation.

3.3   When the yogi who is meditating is only aware of the object of meditation, and no longer aware of self, and only aware of everything as one thing. That is the final step. (Samadhi)

The union of all parts involved. The seer and the seen all become one. In our awareness everything is understood, even if just for a moment. When we are totally content, we are home. When we reach that point in our heads where we feel one hundred percent ok in that place of attention. There is no duality, or this and that, or any desire to be anywhere or have anything else. Do we ever reach this place? I think some do. To me it's like a fleeting moment of bliss, the most amazing feeling of pleasure and love that lasts for a very short time. Like a gift from above to puff our sails, set our compass and send us on our way in the world.

3.4   These three final limbs, concentration, meditation, and union of self and object, create integration.

If you truly want to understand something, use these last three stages of yoga to "integrate" to whatever you're meditating on, whether it's your broken car, new job, or God.

3.5   With the mastery of this integration comes the light of true awareness.

3.6   This practice of integration should be applied in stages, taking your time to understand it.

Don't rush. Slow and steady wins the race here. Awareness comes in layers, in waves. Do a little now and a little later. Take your time. It could take seven minutes or seven lifetimes. Just don't care about it. Practice every day and accept the many great blessings from the practice. There are no goals. There is no black belt, no trophy, and no prize money. Just practice, be happy, and take it as it comes.

3.7   These last three limbs of yoga, concentration, meditation, and union of self and object, are all internal actions, unlike the five before it, which are external actions.

The first five directions in the eight- limbed path are actions that take place in this world, mostly involving our physical selves. The last three are more internal and connected to the action of the soul, not the body. That's why Patanjali ended the descriptions of the first five limbs at the end of the second book, and put the last three limbs in the beginning of book three. He was dividing the external from the internal. For many of us, yoga starts as a physical practice. But over time, we find the mental benefits, and then the spiritual benefits. That's the way it's supposed to happen. First we heal our bodies, then we meet our soul, then we make peace with ourselves and the world. Then, once all those things body and mind have peace, then we have a clean connection for our spirit to connect with the Big-Everything.

3.8   When the true seedless state of union of self and object is reached, even these three final limbs will appear to be external.

In order to understand what we are, we really have to understand what we are "not." Yoga has a really good way of getting us back to realizing our soul. In the final stages of union with the greatest of things, even our own senses and self-awareness will seem to be separate from the soul. The soul just IS. In bliss, there is no philosophy, no practice, no method or guidelines. In the final stage there is only samadhi. Only "is."

3.9   During this practice, thoughts will rise, and be restrained. Mental impressions will come and go, and be restrained. At the moments that your mind restrains these things, transformation occurs.

Every time the mind hands us another thought bubble, we simply say to it "I see you thinking over there, and I get it, but I'm not responding right now." And we go back to our meditating, concentrating. This is how we "restrain" thought. It's not a wrestling match with our minds, it's a recognition that the wisdom and intellect rule over the ego and mind. And we use the authority of our souls to tell our ego, "I'm in charge and we are not wandering our thought there right now." You may have to do this often. It's like a puppy – dedicated, but hard to teach.

3.10   This practice of restraint will clear your mind of unwanted mental impressions, and bring about a flowing, peaceful state.

Over time, it will pay off.

3.11   When we are able to let go of the tendency to focus on many things at once, and learn to focus on one thing, then the consciousness is brought into the state of pure being known as samadhi.

That's the good stuff! That state of pure being is bliss. A calm and controlled mind is the result. Will it last forever? Not likely. But, no worries, we can fix it again. Clean up your mind-stream. Let things get quiet and simple. Let the water of your mind get clear so you can see to the bottom.

3.12   When the coming and going of the waves of the mind are balanced and managed, then the consciousness is transformed to that state of one-pointed awareness.

3.13   Through this action, all things, including elements, the body, and the mind, all go through the process in three stages, starting as true, basic elements, becoming something of character, and ultimately becoming refined.

Here Patanjali takes what seems like a bit of a left turn. What he is doing is hinting to what was accepted physics of his day. All things are subject to the actions of going from a basic element to a molecule, and perhaps being refined into something amazing or unique. We go through something of the same process.

3.14   The pure and basic nature of all things keeps true base properties, whether in a basic state, manifesting into something of character, or settled into a refined state. The true nature of things always stays true.

No matter what we are refined into, our basic elements will always be there. You were always you, and you will always be you.

3.15   The progression through these natural actions of change are what cause distinct changes in our consciousness.

Essentially, this process is the maturity of a human. This process is why we grow mentally. So, to me, yoga is a method to bring us to our maximum maturity, our maximum wisdom potential for ourselves, whatever that is.

3.16   When the yogi begins to understand these three stages of natural progression from basic element, to something with character, to a refined state, then the yogi begins to truly understand past and future.

Understanding this process is going to help us get a really good grasp on why we are the way we are, and how we became that way. In the same light, we will get a handle on where we are going.

3.17   Words, ideas, and objects are all superimposed on the mind. When we restrain them, and subdue their impressions on us, we begin to understand the languages and communications of all living things.

The better we are at thinking without words, the better we will become at communicating without them.

3.18 When the yogi begins to truly understand the deepest of her or his own mental impressions, then they will gain understanding of the origin of their birth, and what the mind was like at the very beginning.

With time and practice, we may be able to trace the construction of our minds back to its origin.

3.19 Then, with this practice, she or he develops deep intuition, and begins to understand the minds of others.

Here, he's not saying you will become a mind-reader. He's saying that you will develop a very keen sense of intuition. I have noticed this to be very true with my own practice.

3.20 With this ability of deep insight, a yogi is even able to see things in the mind of another person that is beyond even that person's awareness.

Again, he's not saying that yogis are mind-readers. He's saying that with this really good intuition you may be able to help others see things in themselves that they are not able to see. Yogis make good counselors, teachers, partners, and friends.

3.21 Yogis shine with awareness, making them attractive and noticeable to others. But, with these abilities intact, a yogi is able to withdraw the shining light from themselves, and blend in, making them appear the same as others, unnoticeable.

A yogi shines with love-light. And when we want to shine, we can shine bright! This is one of the reasons I love teaching yoga. It's a great feeling to be in one place with so many shiny souls! But, we know how to reel it in when we need to. We don't go around smiling and shining to absolutely everyone we meet! We know how to contain it and save it for when it's appropriate.

3.22   It is said that a yogi is also able to control the senses of others, and arrest sound, taste, touch, sight, or smell.

This book of the sutras has a whole list that seems to be super-powers that yogis can attain. Personally, I think that truth is much more logical than that, and that these stories of super-powers that show up in the yogic texts are often nothing more than exaggerations through years of translations. But, I stand firmly in the knowledge that I don't know everything, and I must say that after many years of practice, I have noticed a very deep, almost super-powered intuition, and my ability to understand things has increased many-fold as I have developed my practice. I'm sure that it's this reality that leads to the feeling of super-powers. Later, Patanjali warns against getting too involved with this, because thinking we are super-powered leads to ego, and we get knocked back down a few pegs.

3.23   With this deep intuition developed, yogis may even be able to become fully aware of their own life spans, and the time of their death.

3.24   The yogi who nurtures loving-kindness and compassion towards others gains great moral and emotional strength.

Oh, yes, that's so true. We need this one bad in this world, and if you practice it, it won't be long before you can see the benefits.

3.25   By meditation on the strength and endurance of an elephant, a yogi will gain the strength and endurance of an elephant.

It's not a magic trick. If a person studies an elephant using yoga techniques, she or he will gain a greater understanding of mass and physics, and then be more knowledgeable about such things.

3.26   A yogi will gain the knowledge of concealed things, both near and far.

The more we practice uncovering the truth, uncovering what is concealed, the better we will become at it.

3.27   By meditation on the sun, a yogi can gain knowledge of heaven, hell, and other realms of existence.

3.28   By meditation on the moon, the yogi can gain knowledge or the workings of the cosmos.

3.29   By meditation on the North Star, a yogi can gain knowledge of the future.

3.30   By meditation on the navel of the belly, a yogi can gain knowledge of the systems of the body.

3.31   By meditation on the throat, a yogi can overcome hunger, and thirst.

3.32   By mediation on the throat, a yogi can make her or his body and mind firm and immovable like a large tortoise.

3.33   By mediation on the crown of the head, a yogi can have visions of great and holy beings.

3.34   Through this practice of insight, a yogi can become aware of all knowledge.

3.35   By meditation on the heart, a yogi becomes aware of the nature of consciousness.

3.36   By the practice of meditation, a yogi becomes aware of the difference between the illusion of consciousness, and the truth of the soul.

3.37   Through the practice of this deep intuition, the yogi gains divinely strong senses, which she or he can use at will.

3.38   All these gained abilities are useful in life, but in reality are obstacles to gaining samadhi, the state of pure being.

And there it is. Right in the middle of the list of yogic attributes and super-abilities lies a warning: while these abilities can be useful, getting hung up on them will keep us from realizing our pure being.

3.39   By meditating on, and understanding what causes a person's mind to be bound to the body, it is possible for a yogi to mentally leave the confines of her or his body, and enter and truly understand another person's body.

When we better understand interconnectedness, and we start to understand the relationship between the body and the mind, we become much more empathetic, and we become better healers, listeners, friends, and lovers.

3.40   By meditating on, and understanding how the body transmits information to the mind, a yogi can learn to manage and rise above emotional reactions to stimuli, like being able to tolerate hot or cold water, handle the pain of a thorn, or walk on uncomfortable things barefoot.

We've all seen fire walking. Mind over matter, right?

3.41   With these practices, a yogi begins to radiate a light of love and joy.

3.42   By meditating on sounds, a yogi can gain divine levels of hearing.

3.43   By meditating on the properties of mass and empty space, the yogi gains deep knowledge of the properties of, and what it would feel like, floating through the air.

3.44   By meditating on the existence of the consciousness outside of the body, the yogi destroys the veil that covers the illuminating light of truth.

3.45   The yogi can master the understanding of the elements, in their grossest and most subtle forms, how they interconnect, and what their purposes are, by meditating on them.

3.46   When the understanding of the elements is understood, the yogi is no longer limited by her or his perception of the body, and is capable of amazing things.

3.47   When the body of a yogi is perfected, it will become beautiful, attractive, graceful, hard, and brilliant, like a diamond.

3.48   By meditating on the process of awareness, the ego, and the natural world, a yogi will master the senses.

3.49   Then, the senses will respond and function at the speed of the mind, and the yogi will feel that they have more control over the self, and the natural world.

Keep in mind the original text was written long ago, and they had a very spiritual view of science. What I see when I see these sutras is an heirloom version of psychology and the scientific method.

3.50   Only when the yogi understands the difference between the intellect of the mind, and the one that sees, will she or he understand the truth.

We are not our minds. The seer is not the mind. We see through the mind, not with it. It's easy to say, but hard to wrap our heads around. Meditate on the nature of the mind to find the truth.

3.51   Only by letting go of everything one is bound to, and by renouncing even these gained abilities, can the yogi experience true freedom.

Wow, that's heavy. We can't be free if we are bound, period. If our spirits are attached to worldly things we love or hate, or even attached to being free itself, we can't be free.

3.52   The yogi must beware of becoming attached to great spiritual beings, or seeing self as a great spiritual being, or risk becoming attached to the very obstacles that bound in the first place.

This is a big one for me. We live in a time where everyone rushes to the next Swami Salami or Guru Jane, only to be disappointed to find out, as a result of some scandal, that they are human., and, Disheartened, we move to the next. Or, if we are yoga teachers, we fight and strive and buy trainings and attend workshops and get certifications all to be recognized as a great yoga teacher. But our actions, abilities, and merit speak for themselves. We don't need all that flash to prove it. Find a teacher you like, and can relate to as a person. And be the kind of teacher that guides people to where they are going. I think being humble and seeking humble teachers is really the key here.

3.53   By meditating on time, a yogi can be freed from the mental confines of it.

3.54   With meditation, a yogi can even tell the difference between two things that appear to be alike in all ways.

3.55   The clarity arrived at by these practices is instant and complete, no matter what the object or situation.

Good intuition is often the first thought you have. Wisdom, once firmly rooted, doesn't need to be reasoned out, it just happens in a flash.

3.56   When the mind and soul are both clear and obvious to the perceiver, the yogi has reached the state of total clarity.

In this conclusion of book three, we are again reminded that truth and clarity happen without all this worldly stuff. Teachers, powers, practice, and actions of all kinds are all here. And when we meditate and find the true base materials of mind and soul, we get there, to total clarity.

8
BOOK FOUR: FREEDOM AND LIBERATION

4.1   These spiritual accomplishments can be obtained by being born into the path, through the use of herbs or drugs, by incantation of a spiritual deity, by devotion to a practice, or by meditation.

People all over the world find the truth through many different means. Some are born into the path, ready from birth to become a seeker. Others have a revelation while experimenting with drugs and herbs. I wouldn't say that Patanjali is recommending this method, he's just covering all the bases. Others get to the truth through a spiritual deity like God, Jesus, Buddha, Allah etc. Devoting one's self to a diligent and steady practice can bring us there, if we have an intention the find spiritual truth, whether it's a yoga practice, or even the practice of a sport or instrument. I feel that Patanjali listed meditation last because he put the most value in it.

4.2   Filling one's self with the energy from the natural world brings on a rebirth.

Take a look around at this beautiful world. Sunrises, sparkling waters, and all the amazing details of natural creations remind us how small we are, and how big and beautiful creation is. Reverence is the act of appreciation for the natural world. We look at it and say, "This is a beautiful and good thing and I'm grateful for it." Go out and soak it in, and spend a moment letting is recharge you.

4.3   This great wisdom of yoga does not cause the energy of the natural world to change us, it only allows us to remove obstacles, and create the path, like a farmer who digs an irrigation ditch, guiding the water to the fields.

I love this sutra. When we don't feel well in our soul, when our heart is hurting, we feel like perhaps the good grace of the world is not available to us. But, it is an illusion. The waters of grace and love never stop flowing. Yoga does not create love and grace, it simply teaches us to remove the obstacles and let the goodness flow in.

4.4   The created mind is constructed from the sense of individuality.

It is our perspective that we are an individual that creates our ego. While it is true that you are you and I am me, it is also true that you are me and I am you. When we fully believe that we are separate from each other, our ego behaves as if it were the true us. But, when we wrap our heads around the idea that we are all interconnected, it becomes much easier to see the fine line between the individual ego and the truly interwoven self (soul, atman, parusha).

4.5   Consciousness is only one of the things created by this perspective of individuality. Countless waves of thought and activity come from this idea.

The ego isn't the only thing caused by this misperception of total individuality. The fluctuating waves of the mind, as well as a lot of our chaotic activity, come from this illusion.

4.6   Of these mind waves and activities, only the ones born from the mind in meditation are free from any influence from our dormant mental impressions.

Meditation brings us a clearer mind and a clearer view. We will often find our best-quality thoughts coming out of those moments.

4.7   The actions of people are positive, negative, or neutral in motivation depending on the desired result. The actions of a yogi aim to be pure, transparent, and free from the desire of results.

This is one of those great sutras that is worth re-reading every so often. This one is a big deal. Just about everything we do is motivated by something, and that motivation influences how that action we are doing is going to influence us. A yogi practices doing things without motivation, or without focusing on the motivation. Instead, we practice doing things with a very good intention towards the effort of the action. In other words, we do our best and don't worry about how it will turn out! It may seem odd at first, but with practice this makes great sense. It has a lot to do with learning to surrender to that higher power, whatever that means to you.

4.8   Actions motivated by result leave behind positive, negative, or neutral mental impressions, which will rise up and effect the perception of the person acting, when the conditions are right.

Every time we do something motivated by a result, we plant a little seed in our minds that will later sprout and become a mind wave. The more we act in this way, the more confused and unhappy we become. Do not think that Patanjali is saying don't go and do great things in this world. He is asking you to consider how you treat what you do, and to consider what or who you are really doing it for.

4.9   These impressions of the mind are linked to our memories, and stay linked no matter who we become or how we change.

Memories will always be memories. We love some of our memories, and others we do not like so much. It is important to be mindful of what emotions those memories stir up. Emotions can bring these old mind waves into our heads, and affect our lives today.

4.10   These mental impressions have always existed, because the desire for life and happiness has always existed.

Desire is the root of all motivation. And motivation is the cause of our mental impressions. The more we desire, the more mental chaos we create, and the more likely that we will stumble into ignorance.

4.11   Desire is the cause and mental impressions are the effect. If we let go of the result of our actions, then we let go of this cycle of cause and effect, and break the chain reaction.

If we surrender our desire for results, and practice doing our actions without desire, we will create far less confusion in ourselves. If we practice doing this on a regular basis, we can break some of our bad habits, and start to live in a state that is more peaceful and in-control.

4.12   The past and future are as real as the present. Although the past and future are not in manifest state in the present moment, they still have an effect on our consciousness.

To the mind, there is really no difference between what we are seeing and what we are thinking. Who we are as an individual will always be affected by what we have experienced. Our memories of the past and our fantasies of the future will always affect how we see the world right now.

4.13   The past, present, and future only appear to have different characteristics because of the influence of the three qualities of the natural world. The three qualities are heaviness, activity, and clarity.

The past, present, and future are distinguishably different because of the way our minds view the natural world. We are like little cosmic computers that take in information through the senses, run it through the mind mill processor, and spit out an idea. The qualities of nature act upon all things that we view, whether in our mind's eye, or in front of us. These three qualities are known traditionally as the gunas. The gunas are a reference to more early philosophical pseudo-physics of Patanjali's era. At the time, they perceived nature (prakrati) to consist of three natural influences: (1) tamas, the quality of heaviness, mass, slowness, density, or resistance, (2) rajas, the quality of action, chaos, movement, energy, animation, or thought, and (3) satva, the quality of clarity, transparency, light, open space, or liberty.

4.14   The characteristics of a substance only appear the way they do at any one moment because of the influence of these three qualities of nature. When the qualities of nature change their influence on that thing, it changes.

The matter of this world only seems to be what it is because of the way the gunas are affecting it. This is where we have to say, "Hmm, maybe these old yogis were on to something!" Long before the discovery of particle physics, they knew somehow that the world was made up of energetic "parts," and we only view matter to be what it is because of the way those energetic parts interact.

4.15   The characteristics of an object can appear different depending on the mental state of the person observing it.

We influence what we see. We can all agree that our attitude can change how we see things. We all remember when we were young and our minds would draw monsters in the dark. But Patanjali is also referring to something deeper. Perhaps we actually affect the physical world with our minds. Sounds out-there, but modern physics has suggested very similar theories.

4.16   If the characteristics of an object exist according to the mental state of the person observing it, does that object still exist when not observed?

That's a classic, right? If a tree falls and no one hears it, does it make a sound? Does nature need us to observe it to be what it is? Are we sustaining the physical world with our perception? Again, sounds like madness, but some modern theories suggest it.

4.17   Whether an object is known or unknown depends on the mental state and expectations of the mind of the observer.

We don't see what we don't understand, and sometimes we don't see what we don't want to see.

4.18   The soul is always awake and aware. Being that the mind is a tool used by the soul for observation, the soul is always aware of the fluctuations and actions of the mind.

Although we often forget, the soul is always there. The soul always knows what the mind is doing.

4.19   The mind is able to be perceived by the soul. The mind has no awareness of its own.

A reminder that the soul has awareness, and the mind does not.

4.20   The mind can create ideas and images, but the soul observes them. The mind cannot be both the presenter and receiver of these ideas and images.

If we can observe our minds, then where is that observation coming from? It has to be something other than mind.

4.21   If the mind were both presenter and receiver of these ideas and images, then our memories would not be possible – with no separate source of memory and awareness, how could memories be recalled at will?

The mind is the movie screen. The soul is sitting in the theater.

4.22   When the mind is not reflecting an external object, and we become aware of the soul, then the mind becomes clear and reflects the soul.

Like clear, calm water, the mind reflects the soul back at itself, allowing the soul to be aware of the soul. Mind waves create choppy water, preventing the reflection of awareness of the true self.

4.23   The mind is able to be aware in two ways, first by observing an object and presenting it to the soul, and second, by reflecting the soul for the purpose of self-awareness and understanding.

Since the mind has no awareness of its own, there are two ways it participates in awareness. First, by combining the senses and feeding an image or information to the soul; and second, by reflecting the soul back at itself, just like in the reflecting pool described above.

4.24   The mind is filled with impressions that influence its functions. But the mind serves the soul because of its proximity to the soul, and to the natural world, like a translator.

Even though the mind is far from perfect and may not always serve us as we would like, it is very important to us. The mind serves as the one true connection between our spiritual bodies and our physical bodies.

4.25   A yogi who has reached a state of clarity and peace no longer desires to understand the perceiver known as the soul.

No longer having the seeker's desire is a good indicator that you are getting a good grasp on your own soul. It means that you are getting to know yourself and becoming really ok with that.

4.26   And in that beautiful state of awareness of the soul, the yogi only craves one thing, to remain in that place of pure freedom.

In truth there is no confusion. We only attach to the truth.

4.27   Although unlikely, it is possible that the yogi can regress from this awareness, and past impressions of the mind can take hold, again dividing the awareness of the soul from the mind.

There is no guarantee that once you are clear-minded and connected that you will stay there. We have to remain diligent in order to stay connected.

4.28   A yogi must work to overcome the impressions that divide the mind and soul, in the same way one works to overcome the five great obstacles.

The five obstacles are covered again as we keep reading.

4.29   A yogi who reaches the highest state of clarity, and has let go of all the desires and longing, will feel the grace of supreme love come down like rain.

Just breathe that in for a second. Let it sit with you. Let it speak to your heart. Let it water your soul.

4.30   This is indeed the life free from actions based on ignorance, ego, attachment, aversion, and the fear of death.

A yoga life is a life free from those five obstacles.

4.31   When the mind is free from the clouds of misperception, there is nothing left to be understood.

Once we're there, we're done. It may not last, but in that head state, we have no more work to do.

4.32   When we are free, the three characteristics of the natural world – heaviness, activity, and clarity – no longer draw us into the cycle of pleasure and pain.

The three gunas – the churning, changing forces of nature – no longer rule over us. Pleasure and pain no longer rule over us.

4.33   As these three characteristics of nature no longer effect the yogi, the awareness of the passing of time loses its power.

Time itself no longer rules over us. We realize the eternal nature of soul.

4.34   When the highest goal in life is reached, and we are truly free, and the pattern of heaviness, activity, and clarity no longer rule us, the soul sees clearly through the mind, without misperception.

We see the final and total truth. We have true freedom, released from bondage. We are at peace. We settle into the Big-Everything, the union of all the parts, the wholeness, the yoga.

Take away what you need from the sutras. Then go out and practice, practice, practice. Re-read it, talk about it, think about it, and re-read it again. Read other versions and other texts that feed your soul. Put it into action in your life. Let it bring you to the best of yourself. Get better connected. Develop real connection with your family, friends, church, or community. Get involved. And most of all, stay free.

9
SIMPLE MEDITATION

It can be a bit of a challenge going from a place of deep philosophy to a place of simple meditation. I've found that it's nice to have some basic outlines to work from. Here is a general and simple direction to meditation:

- Work out the kinks in your body.
- Sit in a comfortable position.
- Close your eyes.
- Sit up tall and aware.
- Become familiar with your breathing.
- Drop the past and future.
- Get into the moment, everything about it. Become aware of all the senses.
- BUT, don't judge the senses. Don't let them start a story or idea in your "mind mill."
- Realize your simple, true nature.

Feel free to ad or mix ideas into your meditations, to help get you where you are going. Try adding a focus, like gazing into a candle or meditating on a sunset. If you have a religious background, simply be present with the Creator.

Don't become discouraged. Keep practicing. It will get easier and more enjoyable the more you practice. At first it may be no fun at all, but the benefits will keep us going. In no time it will be something you crave.

Keep your meditation simple, easy, light, and loving. Take your time to grow into who you really are. Keep moving forward with love. Slow, strong, and steady.

ABOUT THE AUTHOR

Mathew "Huck" Ingles is dedicated to the field of yoga. With over 20 years of practice, he has established himself as a successful yoga teacher, well known for his down-to-earth classes and workshops, which combine a solid workout with practical yoga philosophy and a wild sense of humor.

Huck lives in Savona, NY with his wife Angela and their son Eli. He spends his time farming, hiking, traveling, and enjoying the natural beauty of the Finger Lakes.

Currently, Huck teaches regular yoga classes in the Finger Lakes region of New York. He also offers workshops and organizes yoga events throughout New York State and beyond. Huck is the founder and director of the Finger Lakes Yoga Festival.

To learn more about Huck, his workshops, events, or classes, visit his website at:
www.huckleberryyoga.com

For book orders, reviews, and information, visit:
www.simplesutras.com

Made in the USA
Lexington, KY
15 May 2019